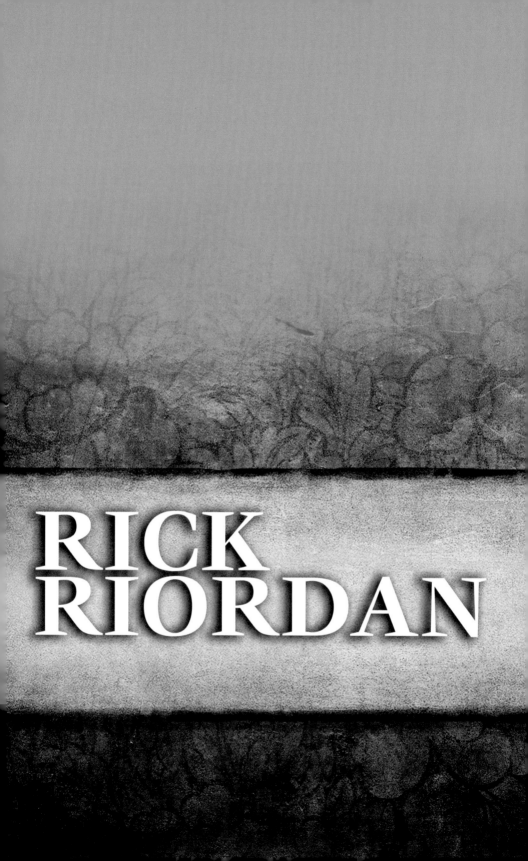

RICK RIORDAN

RICK RIORDAN

ADAM FURGANG

ROSEN
PUBLISHING®

New York

Dedicated to Ben—Keep on reading!

Published in 2013 by The Rosen Publishing Group, Inc.
29 East 21st Street, New York, NY 10010

Library of Congress Cataloging-in-Publication Data

Furgang, Adam.
Rick Riordan/Adam Furgang.—1st ed.
    p. cm.—(All about the author)
Includes bibliographical references and index.
ISBN 978-1-4488-6937-4 (library binding)
1. Riordan, Rick—Juvenile literature. 2. Authors, American—20th century—Biography—Juvenile literature. I. Title.
PS3568.I5866Z67 2012
813'.6—dc23
[B]
                                                    2011044131

Manufactured in the United States of America

CPSIA Compliance Information: Batch #S12YA: For further information, contact Rosen Publishing, New York, New York, at 1-800-237-9932.

CONTENTS

In February of 2010, fans of *The Lightning Thief*—the first volume in author Rick Riordan's Percy Jackson and the Olympians series of young adult novels—swarmed movie theaters across the United States to view the movie adaptation. The film earned $58.7 million in its first two weeks. While that's a good showing for a movie, its popularity sparked an even more spectacular event. All five books in the Riordan's Percy Jackson series reached *USA Today's* top ten list during the same week. Ticket sales drove up book sales for the rest of the series, and Riordan (rhymes with "fire den") became more popular than ever.

With Riordan's Kane Chronicles, The 39 Clues, and the Heroes of Olympus series in the works, there was a lot riding on the success of the Percy Jackson books and film adaptations. The Percy Jackson and the Olympians series was sparking young people's interest in ancient Greek mythology. The gods and demigods of the Greek world were being brought into modern times by Riordan's stories, and teens and preteens were loving it.

Similarly, once published, the Kane Chronicles sparked teens' interest in Egyptian mythology. The 39 Clues series was created along with Scholastic Books and became an instant hit, with film adaptations in the works as well. Toys and games

Rick Riordan attends events where he can meet with fans and sign his latest books. His novels have sold millions of copies around the world.

surrounding all of these series have been sold every-
where. Everything Rick Riordan works on seems
to be devoured instantly by eager young people all
around the world who are willing to learn and are
excited to hear a great story well told.

So how did someone who grew up as a reluctant
reader, someone who didn't like books, go on to find
such enormous success as a writer and storyteller?
As a child, Riordan thought books were too difficult
to read and, in the end, not very interesting or worth
the effort. At first, he wasn't one of those kids who
would eagerly devour book after book and become
lost in elaborate fictional worlds spread across entire
series. It wasn't until Riordan was in middle school
that he gained an interest in reading. Yet today, he is
one of the most popular and well-loved young adult
authors in North America and worldwide.

While Riordan did eventually grow to love both
reading and writing, it was a long journey for him.
When he noticed his own young son struggling with
reading, Riordan was able to capture his attention
in the same way that he had finally been hooked—
through an interest in the otherworldly appeal of
mythology. It was from these bedtime stories that
he told to his son that the Percy Jackson series
was born.

The series not only helped capture his son's
imagination, it also started a very successful career

for Riordan as a young adult writer. Today, not only do Percy Jackson fans eagerly await another movie installment of the best-selling books, but increasing hype surrounds the film adaptations of the Kane Chronicles and the 39 Clues, too. But behind all of these impressive tokens of fame and success lie very humble beginnings. The stories millions of children love today came from the mind of just one man. One man who was trying to put his son to bed at night and get him interested in school can be thanked for the success of Percy Jackson, Kane Chronicles, the 39 Clues, and the Heroes of Olympus series.

ONE

A PORTRAIT OF THE ARTIST AS A YOUNG MAN

Rick Riordan was born on June 5, 1964, in San Antonio, Texas. He was born into a family of creative teachers. His mother taught high school art, but she also had a passion for music. His father taught vocational technology (vo-tech) but loved making ceramics. Vo-tech classes help high school students learn a specific trade, like plumbing, welding, construction, auto mechanics, electronics, or information technology. Even Riordan's grandparents were teachers. With all of these teachers and creative people in his family, it's no wonder Riordan grew up to eventually become first a teacher and then a fiction writer.

TOLKIEN OVERCOMES A RELUCTANT READER

Rick Riordan was a quiet and thoughtful child. According to an interview with AdLit.org, Riordan said about his childhood, "I would be more likely to play with Legos or build robots or make imaginary worlds than I was to be outside tossing a football around." One might assume, given his solitary and quiet nature, that Riordan was interested in reading as a child. After all, he was imaginative, would eventually become a writer and teacher, and was even raised by teachers. Ironically, however, Riordan did not enjoy reading when he was very young. He was what might be referred to as a "late bloomer" in terms of reading. As a young child, he found that books bored him more than they interested him. He could not relate to the stories he read or the characters that he read about.

Riordan's middle school years finally opened his eyes to the rich creative and imaginative possibilities of literature. The first books that Riordan could remember really enjoying were those in the *Lord of the Rings* trilogy. The fantasy series, written by J. R. R. Tolkien, is one of the most

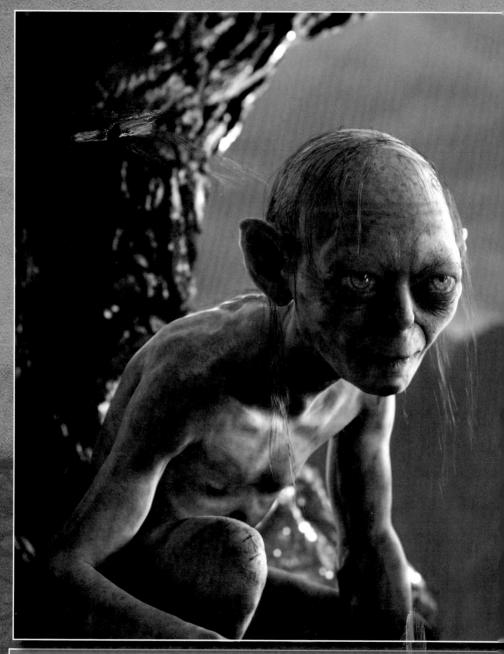

The Lord of the Rings trilogy by J. R. R. Tolkien was the first reading experience Riordan could remember enjoying as a child. The books were later made into blockbuster Hollywood movies. Gollum, shown here, was one of the characters in the film.

famous and well-loved fantasy sagas of all time. The epic tale follows a group of unlikely heroes as they struggle to destroy a powerful ring and its creator before the entire world is destroyed by their evil power.

Riordan could not put these books down, a new experience for him as a reader. Before encountering Tolkien, he found reading to be a struggle and a chore. No story had captured his attention like *The Lord of the Rings*. The three books in the trilogy, *The Fellowship of the Ring*, *The Two Towers*, and *The Return of the King*, were published in the 1950s. They continued and expanded upon the story first started in Tolkien's 1937 novel *The Hobbit*. In this complex saga, the heroes were loveable, flawed, and fascinating, and the villains were evil but darkly captivating. The series—and the fictional, fantastical world created by it—riveted Riordan's attention and made him excited about reading for the first time.

When he was finished reading *The Lord of the Rings* trilogy, a new door had been opened for him. According to his personal Web site, Riordan remembers that around the same time he was discovering Tolkien, he was also inspired by his middle school English teacher, Mrs. Pabst. She

NORSE MYTHOLOGY

Norse mythology dates back to the days before Christianity. These Scandinavian, Anglo-Saxon, and Germanic stories explain many of the mysteries of our natural world. One such story tells how the world was created. According to the myth, an ice world existed on one end of the earth, and a land of fire existed on the other. In between these two worlds was a vast emptiness. It was in this emptiness that many of the creatures of mythology existed. Giant trolls, dwarves, six-headed monsters, gods and children of gods, and eventually, the first humans were created in this "middle-earth."

revealed to him that Tolkien's stories actually have their roots in Norse mythology. Riordan had been unaware of this but quickly became fascinated by the ancient Scandinavian and Germanic folklore and tried to learn as much as he could about it.

Written versions of Norse myths and sagas date back to the 1200s. Like other cultures' similar folkloric traditions, Norse mythology features stories of gods and goddesses with special powers. It has influenced many kinds of fantasy writing that came after it. For example, a direct inspiration for *The Lord of the Rings* may have been the *draupnir*, which is a magic golden arm ring made by dwarves for the father of the gods, Odin. The ring's name means "the dripper." It provided endless wealth to whoever had it because eight new rings would drip from it on every ninth morning. In *The Lord of the Rings*, a magical ring took possession of anyone who touched it. In both tales, the rings represented greed, evil, and ruin among the humans who tried to possess them for their own.

As Riordan learned more about world mythology in middle school and high school, the more inspiration and background he would have for his writing as an adult.

A GROWING INTEREST IN WRITING

Mrs. Pabst's influence on Riordan did not stop with introducing him to Norse mythology. She also encouraged his writing. She must have noticed some natural talent in Riordan and encouraged him to submit his writing to a literary magazine. With his first submission at age thirteen, however, Riordan received his first rejection letter. The story was never published, but, undaunted, Riordan's love of writing continued to grow through the years.

Riordan attended high school in San Antonio, Texas, at Alamo Heights High. He worked on the school newspaper as an editor, and his feature writing won him a third-place prize in a state competition. He did a little writing "off the record" as well, and published an

This painting, *Ride of the Valkyrie*, by William T. Maud, depicts the gods of Norse mythology traveling to Valhalla, which is ruled by the god Odin. Riordan was greatly influenced by Norse mythology, and it continues to be a theme in some of his most popular books.

underground newspaper, which is one that is not approved by the school. The articles made fun of the school instead of reporting straight news and school spirit pieces like traditional school newspapers did. His favorite target to poke fun at was the football team's losing record. He eventually got into trouble for his work on this underground newspaper. The football team even egged his car in retaliation for his mockery. But the writing bug had already taken hold in Riordan. By the time he got to college, he was well on his way to making writing one of his favorite pastimes.

When it came time to choose which college to go to, however, Riordan chose the University of North Texas because of its music program. Riordan applied to the school because he wanted to major in music and become a guitar player. However, he eventually transferred to the University of Texas at Austin. At UT-Austin, Riordan's major changed to two of his great interests—English and history.

A LOVE OF MUSIC, A LOVE OF BOOKS

Riordan worked his way through college by performing a rather unusual job. He played in a rock and roll band! He even looked the part. He sported long hair with a beard and mustache, closely resembling the rock stars of the 1970s and 1980s. The band performed classic songs by the Beatles and the Rolling Stones, but they also performed some of their own music. Riordan felt that writing songs provided valuable skills and experience to a storyteller and literary author. Writing song lyrics helped Riordan understand what made some lines sound better than others and appreciate the importance of word choice, images, and construction.

Riordan enjoyed playing the guitar and may have gotten some of his musical talent from his mother, who also loved to play music. Even though Riordan did not end up majoring in music and playing the guitar for a living, he still enjoyed playing in the band and his love of music influenced his choice of colleges.

Riordan's love for writing and reading grew a lot in college, especially because of his concentration in English. He admits that he did not read all of the books he was assigned to read in high school. He felt that he had a natural ability to write what was expected of him in reports. He would listen in class and then write his papers without having actually read the books. When he later became a teacher, he of course recommended that his students do not skip the readings they were assigned. In

Riordan attended the University of Texas at Austin. It was here that he gained a great interest in reading, literature, and history.

fact, when Riordan went to college, he returned to those classic books he didn't read in high school and read them all out of curiosity and a growing love of literature. During his college years, he became so interested in reading that he tried to read everything he could get his hands on. It was quite a switch from the young boy who could not get interested in the books around him.

After graduating from the University of Texas at Austin, Riordan decided to use his double major in English and history to become a teacher. He went to the University of Texas at San Antonio to get his teaching degree in English and history. While he was studying in San Antonio, Riordan got his first pieces of writing published (not counting his articles for the high school newspaper). He wrote two short stories that appeared in UT-San Antonio's literary magazine.

After completing his student teaching in San Antonio, Riordan was on his way to starting his teaching career, which he thoroughly enjoyed and still misses sometimes—even today.

CHAPTER TWO

BECOMING A WRITER

Rick Riordan worked as a student teacher in San Antonio, Texas, and received his teaching degree. He got his first teaching job at a middle school in New Braunfels, Texas. Soon after beginning his career, however, Riordan moved to San Francisco, California, with his wife, Becky. They lived there for eight years, and Riordan taught at Presidio High School.

FULL-TIME TEACHER, PART-TIME WRITER

Riordan greatly enjoyed teaching and began to think about what it was that made a good teacher. He knew it had a lot to do with meeting the needs of the students he taught. "They needed somebody

to take them seriously," he said in an interview with AdLit.org. "They needed somebody not to waste their time. They wanted to come into the classroom and feel like the teacher knew what they were doing and cared about them and had structured the lesson in a way that would engage them with the informa-tion. And that took a long time for me to realize that that was part of my job—was to really be as excited about learning as I expected my kids to be." He wanted his students to love learning and reading, and he felt it was his job to inspire that love and share his own passion for reading, writing, and literature. "If I turn them off to reading," he said in the interview, "if they left my room thinking that English was bor-ing, then I hadn't done my job."

In addition to trying to inspire his students, Riordan also worked on his own writing in his spare time. He had been a fan of mystery novels since

Riordan's experience as a middle school teacher gave him special insight into what young readers find interesting and entertaining. This knowledge—and a classroom full of brutally honest critics—honed his skills as a storyteller and helped make him the wildly successful and popular writer he is today.

college. According to an interview with Scholastic, he was also a little bit homesick for San Antonio, Texas, so he wrote a story about a detective named Tres Navarre who lived and worked in that city. The setting of the story was very familiar to Riordan, so he didn't have to do a lot of background research to make his story believable. Most important, it allowed him to write about his beloved hometown.

Riordan spent many months waking up early to be able to write before heading off to work at Presidio High. He submitted a completed manuscript to publishers but soon received many rejection letters. It was the fourteenth publisher to receive the manuscript, Bantam Doubleday Dell, that finally accepted the work. Riordan finished writing the book in June of 1994, just before he turned thirty years old.

It was not until three years later, in 1997, that *Big Red Tequila* was finally published. Riordan admits that even with this long wait between finished work and finished book, he was one of the lucky few. Most other writers wait a much longer period of time for their work to be published, if they get published at all. Regardless of the long wait, Bantam Doubleday Dell's offer gave Riordan inspiration to continue writing.

Riordan was so inspired by writing, in fact, that he turned the Tres Navarre novel into a detective series. He has published seven more adult books since Navarre's debut in *Big Red Tequila*, writing a book each year for that series. At the time he began the Tres Navarre series, Riordan did not think about writing for children. He enjoyed reading adult books, so that's also what he wrote. It did not cross his mind to write for children until years later.

After Riordan and his wife had their two sons, Haley and Patrick, they moved back to San Antonio for good after being in San Francisco for eight years. Riordan began teaching sixth, seventh, and eighth grade English and social studies at Saint Mary's Hall in San Antonio. He enjoyed the work and especially loved teaching his students about world mythology.

PERCY JACKSON IS BORN

It was not until Riordan's son Haley began having trouble learning to read that the idea of Percy Jackson occurred to the author of adult detective fiction. Riordan's son enjoyed the Greek mythology that his second grade class was studying. This was the first time Haley showed any interest in school, where he was struggling. To stoke Haley's newfound interest, Riordan began telling him bedtime stories centering upon Greek myths. This ploy worked better than expected. Haley asked Riordan to tell him more bedtime stories about the Greek gods. He did this for a while until he ran out of stories to tell. At

Riordan wasn't the only person influenced by Greek myths. Artists and architects have been influenced by ancient mythology for centuries. This sculpture of Neptune appears in Venice, Italy.

that point, Haley asked his father to make up some new stories using the classic characters with whom he was already familiar.

As Riordan states on his Web site: "I thought about it for a few minutes. Then I remembered a creative writing project I used to do with my sixth graders—I would let them create their own demigod hero, the son or daughter of any god they wanted, and have them describe a Greek-style quest for that hero." This is what caused Riordan to invent the character of Percy Jackson, who is the demigod son of Poseidon, god of the sea. In his made-up story, Percy had to find Zeus's lightning bolt in modern-day America. "It took about three nights to tell the whole story," Riordan recalled, "and when I was done, Haley told me I should write it out as a book." Even though Riordan was teaching full-time and, in his spare time, writing novels in the Tres Navarre series, he also found time to begin work on the Percy Jackson story over the next year.

Riordan felt a special desire to finish the story for his son. It was during the time that the book was being written that his son was increasingly having trouble focusing in school and learning to read. When he was brought to be tested for learning disabilities, it was found that he had dyslexia and attention deficit/hyperactivity disorder (ADHD).

Dyslexia is a disability in which letters, words, numbers, or other symbols may appear jumbled or out of order, making it difficult to read. ADHD is a disability that often occurs in children, in which they have trouble concentrating and may demonstrate hyperactive behavior, including very high energy levels and poor impulse control. The two disabilities are often diagnosed together because the inability to interpret letters and symbols correctly can often frustrate children and make it difficult for them to concentrate when they are asked. This, in turn, makes it more likely for them to engage in avoidance behavior that takes them off-task.

It was because of Haley's experience with dyslexia and ADHD that Riordan chose to give his Percy Jackson character these same disabilities. He felt it was something that not only his son but also many other young readers with the same challenges could relate to. People with dyslexia or ADHD are often misunderstood and viewed as lazy or unintelligent. In fact, they are often quite intelligent, and they are forced to think in creative, innovative, and unconventional ways because they have to find ways to learn despite their disabilities. "Making Percy ADHD/dyslexic was my way of honoring the potential of all the kids I've known who have those conditions," Riordan explains in an interview posted on his Web site. "It's not a bad thing to be different. Sometimes, it's the mark of being very, very talented. That's what Percy discovers about himself in *The Lightning Thief*."

TESTING THE WATERS

It took Riordan months of writing to come up with the story that became the first book in the Percy Jackson and the Olympians series: *The Lightning Thief*. When it was finished, he read it to his sons, who loved it. He then felt it was time to let some of his seventh and eighth grade students read it.

Riordan admits that he was nervous about letting his students read the book because he knew they would be tough critics. But he was relieved when they liked the book. He said that they gave him great feedback, such as the idea that he needed to change the title. "The first title was *Son of the Sea God*," he said in an interview with AdLit. org, "and the kids said: no, no, no—you can't call it that because it gives away who his father is too early." In an interview on Riordan's Web site, he further explained how the novel was refined by the thoughtful comments of his students: "They also had some good ideas on how Percy should act if he had ADHD. One student helped me refine the way Percy's sword, Anaklusmos, worked. I'm very glad I showed the novel to kids first. After all, that's who it's written for."

In addition to his students and his son Haley, the character of Percy Jackson was also directly inspired and shaped by Rick Riordan himself. Riordan claims that Percy Jackson's sense of humor and mediocre grades were similar to his own.

CONNECTING WITH HIS AUDIENCE

Some inspirations for the Percy Jackson books came from other aspects of Riordan's life. For instance, Camp Half-Blood, the training camp for demigods, was inspired by a real experience in Riordan's life. He got the idea for Camp Half-Blood from his three years spent working as a music director

at a summer camp in Texas called Camp Capers. A specialized camp for students with specific

Riordan talks about reading and writing to a group of fifth and sixth graders in Austin, Texas. Now a full-time writer, Riordan enjoys the opportunity to get back into the classroom and discuss literature with students whenever possible.

interests and abilities appealed to Riordan, and he kept the idea in mind until he found a way to use it in the Percy Jackson books.

It was extremely important to Riordan, as he was writing, to connect with his audience and constantly think of the children and teens who would be reading his books. Just as he thought his job as a teacher was to keep kids interested, intrigued, and inspired, he felt he had to fulfill the same tasks as a writer. "When I was writing Percy Jackson," he explained in his AdLit.org interview, "I saw my sixth grade class in front of me. I imagined myself reading the manuscript to my fifth period class after lunch; and any classroom teacher can tell you that's a pretty tough litmus test. If you can keep them engaged fifth period after lunch, you know you're doing something right." Riordan tested his writing with an even tougher audience as well, one closer to home: "And I read it aloud to my own sons to make sure that it wasn't going to slow down, that it didn't lose their interest, and if they started drifting away, I would change that passage until I knew that I had their attention all the way through."

All of the thought that Riordan put into his work helped make the Percy Jackson books successful. He also credits Greek mythology as a surefire way to grab and keep a young reader's attention, with

GET TO KNOW THE GREEK GODS

The gods in the Percy Jackson and the Olympians series are the same gods that form the pantheon of Greek mythology. Here is a list of the most well-known gods from Greek mythology and those that play key roles in the Percy Jackson series. The first are the three brothers, Poseidon, Zeus, and Hades, each of whom rules a separate part of the world.

- Poseidon is the god of the sea. He carries a long stake with three arrows at the end, called a trident. He can cause storms and earthquakes by shaking the earth with his trident.
- Zeus is known as the ultimate god of the Olympians. He is god of the sky and ruler of all humankind. He causes all weather and therefore should be thanked for fair weather and feared in stormy weather.
- Hades is the god of the underworld and of the dead. He uses a helmet to stay invisible. The symbol of Cerberus—a three-headed dog that guards the entrance to the underworld—represents him.
- Athena is the goddess of wisdom, war, and skill. She is the daughter of Zeus and was born by springing right out of Zeus's head. She emerged fully formed and grown to adulthood and wearing body armor.

its abundance of magic, monsters, action, mystery, adventure, and fascinatingly flawed heroes. It also helps that the demigods Riordan writes about have a connection to the typical middle school student. In his interview with AdLit.org, Riordan explains why so many middle school students enjoy reading about Greek mythology and the demigods of the Percy Jackson and the Olympians series. He explains: "Your typical Greek hero is half-God, half-man, and they're sort of stuck in between worlds. They don't really fit in in either place; and yet they have all these Herculean challenges that they have to overcome. And I think a middle school kid feels kind of like that. They're not really an adult, they're not really a kid." Just as the heroes in the stories are facing difficult challenges while straddling and shuttling between two worlds, so, too, are middle school students.

Riordan increased the inherent interest of the mythological material by bringing it into the modern era. Set in contemporary times, Percy Jackson comes to realize that not only are the Greek myths and gods real, but they still exist today. Instead of the Twelve Olympians dwelling on Mount Olympus, they now live on the six hundredth floor of New York City's Empire State Building, which is a semi-mythical place itself in the world's imagination. The characters in the first Percy Jackson book, *The*

Riordan's first book for children, *The Lightning Thief*, was published in 2005 and made into a Hollywood film in 2010. The movie starred Logan Lerman as Percy Jackson.

Lightning Thief, visit legendary places in the United States—such as Las Vegas, the American Museum of Natural History in New York, the Hollywood Hills—where they encounter and interact with the gods and goddesses of the Greek world.

GOING HOLLYWOOD

Not only did Riordan's children and students enjoy the first book in the Percy Jackson series, but publishers did, too. In 2005, *The Lightning Thief* was published by Miramax Books, which was the publishing arm of Miramax Films, a production company started by Bob and Harvey Weinstein, famous film producers. So interest in adapting the Percy Jackson books for film was in the works early on. After the book was published, the Miramax Books division became part of its parent company, the Walt Disney Company. The Percy Jackson books are now published under the name Disney Hyperion.

With *The Lightning Thief* selling fast and a movie deal in the works, Riordan was on his way to making Percy Jackson into a five-book series, with one book to be published each year. Both Percy Jackson and Rick Riordan would soon become stars.

WHEN LIGHTNING STRIKES: HITTING THE BIG TIME

U ntil Rick Riordan's Percy Jackson series was sold to publishers, Riordan had been living a fairly normal life. While he still published a new adult-oriented Tres Navarre detective novel about once a year, he was teaching full-time. He could only write his Navarre books in his spare time. But all of that would change in 2005, when the first book in the five-book Percy Jackson and the Olympians series, *The Lightning Thief*, was published.

LEAVING THE CLASSROOM

According to his Web site, Riordan knew that after the Percy Jackson books became popular, he would no longer have the time to teach and write at the same time: "When I sold the Percy Jackson series to Disney

As a published, popular author who has sold millions of copies of his books world-wide, Rick Riordan is now able to inspire far more students than he could when he taught only a lucky few as a middle school instructor. One of the things he loves most about being a published author is the opportunity it has provided him to pass along his love of learning and literature to millions of schoolchildren worldwide.

Book Group, I realized that I'd now have to write two books a year to keep up with my deadlines—one adult book, and one children's book. I just didn't think I'd be able to keep up that pace and do a good job in the classroom, so I made the reluctant decision to leave teaching."

For years after he quit teaching, Riordan went on many school visits to give talks as an author. He enjoyed staying in touch with students in this way. However, he admitted in an interview with AdLit.org that there were parts about being a teacher that he missed. "I miss having my own students and getting to know them over the course of the year and knowing their names and watching them grow up and having them come back the next year." But Riordan realized that there were also benefits to reaching a lot of kids at once through his books, rather than just one class at a time. He states on his Web site, "Hopefully, I'll be able to get more kids interested in reading mythology with my books than I ever did as a teacher."

MOVIEMAKING

The film studio 20th Century Fox ended up purchasing the movie rights to the first Percy Jackson book, *The Lightning Thief*. The film was directed by Chris Columbus, who directed many blockbuster

The actors from the movie *Percy Jackson & the Olympians: The Lightning Thief* appear from left to right: Kevin McKidd, Brandon T. Jackson, Pierce Brosnan, Alexandra Daddario, and Logan Lerman, with director Chris Columbus.

Hollywood movies, including *Harry Potter and the Sorcerer's Stone* and *Harry Potter and the Chamber of Secrets*.

It was exciting for Riordan to know that a director with such a keen understanding of action and children's literature would be handling the movie adaptation of his book. He allowed the movie details to be handled by the moviemakers because he realized that is the job they are good at. He is a writer, not a filmmaker, so he resisted the temptation to meddle and he let the pros do their job. He admitted in an interview with AdLit.org that he would not know how to go about writing a screenplay. "And even if I were to try," he said, "I don't think I would have time to do it well." He understood that there were bound to be differences between the book and the movie. "They always have to change

Logan Lerman, who played the role of Percy Jackson in the film *Percy Jackson & the Olympians: The Lightning Thief*, signs autographs for fans. Brandon T. Jackson, who played Grover, and Alexandra Daddario, who played Annabeth, sit next to him.

books when they turn them into movies because there's simply no way that you can take everything in a 350-page book and present it accurately in two hours."

On Scholastic.com's book blog, *The Stacks*, Riordan explained to Percy Jackson fans that they should expect some changes from the book. He warned his readers: "Movies are a totally different medium. What you'll be seeing is not *The Lightning Thief* book copied page for page onto the screen. What you'll be seeing is Chris Columbus's interpretation of *The Lightning Thief* story… Let the movie be the movie, and the books be the books, and try to enjoy the story without getting too worked up about any differences."

The actors in the film also thought the differences between the book and the movie made sense.

Logan Lerman, who played Percy, was interviewed by *The Stacks* and he commented on the film adaptation: "I'm pretty sure that fans of the book will be able to appreciate Rick's writing and will still accept this as a different medium from the book that adds a whole different take on the book from another person's eyes, from Chris Columbus's vision." He said that turning the book into a film "even makes it more grand, even more unique. It's really cool."

Brandon T. Jackson, the actor who played Grover in the film, also spoke to *The Stacks* and explained that people have to separate the book from the movie: "You'll get some flak from a lot of the kids who will say, 'I didn't expect Grover to look like this.' 'I didn't expect Alexander to look like this.' But when you take it for the entertainment value, I think the movie comes out to be really, really cool."

Apparently, fans of *The Lightning Thief* were able to accept the film version on its own terms and did indeed find it to be really cool. The movie made $226 million worldwide, and a movie adaptation of the second book, *The Sea of Monsters*, quickly went into development with most of the same actors on board. Columbus was expected to produce rather than direct the second film. *The Lightning Thief* movie also inspired tie-in action figures and a Nintendo DS video game.

THE LIGHTNING THIEF: THE BOOK VS. THE MOVIE

As with any book-to-screen adaptation, there are differences between the two versions of *The Lightning Thief*. Here is a list of some of the differences between the book and movie versions of the first installment of the Percy Jackson series:

- In the book, Percy and Annabeth are twelve years old, but in the movie they are seventeen.
- In the book, Percy is given three pearls as a gift from his father, and Percy takes them to the Underworld. In the movie, the pearls were Persephone's, and they are used to help visitors escape the Underworld. Percy must go to three locations in the United States to find them and rescue his mom.
- In the book, Percy does not yet have his shield wristwatch because he does not get it from Tyson until the second book. In the movie, however, he already has a shield, given to him by Luke.
- In the book, the Oracle sends Percy on quests and makes prophecies, but in the movie there is no Oracle.
- In the book, Percy can barely control his powers, but in the movie he can control them. In the book series, it is not until the fourth installment, *The Battle of the Labyrinth*, that Percy has such command over his abilities.
- In the book, Ares has a major role, but in the movie, he only appears when the gods are fighting

with each other.

▪In the book, Hydra does not appear until *The Sea of Monsters*, but Hydra appears in the film version of *The Lightning Thief*.

▪In the book, the Big House plays an important role, but in the movie it is never shown or mentioned.

A BEST-SELLING SERIES

The Percy Jackson and the Olympians series was just the beginning of Rick Riordan's success. In the next couple of years, he would have Percy Jackson novels on the *New York Times* best-seller lists and fans eagerly waiting for new books in the series to be released. He found it very important to keep up with the publisher's writing schedules and deadlines so that the books would keep coming out on time. Any large gaps between release of the novels may cause readers to lose interest and move on.

A full-time author must carve a schedule out for himself or herself. In an interview with AdLit. org, Riordan explained the schedule he developed when he became a full-time author. He said: "If I'm at home, I'll get up in the morning, and I'll usually do a little bit of writing; and then I will stop when the kids get up and my sons are ready to go to school—I'll get them off to school, I'll take care of some business; and then I'll go back to the writing in the afternoon."

Riordan also explained in the interview that you have to work when it's best for you. He stated: "I tend to work best around the edges of the day and the early morning or late at night when the house is quiet, and my mind seems to work best then. And I'd like to say that I write eight hours a day—I don't. I usually write about two or three hours a day maximum; and I find that, after that, I just get diminishing returns, and I just am not able to do much more than that."

By the time *The Lightning Thief* was released in movie theaters on February 12, 2010, the Percy Jackson and the Olympians series was at the height of its popularity. The movie earned $57.8 million in its first two weeks of release, and all five of the books in the series were on *USA Today's* top ten list of children's books in the same week.

Each time a book in the series was released in bookstores, a larger and larger number of copies were printed. Usually a publisher will try not to

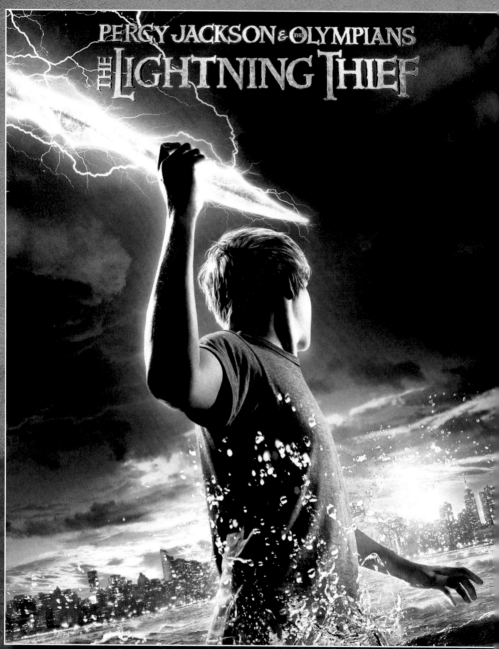

This is the official movie poster for *Percy Jackson & the Olympians: The Lightning Thief*. When the movie came out in 2010, the Percy Jackson series was at the height of its popularity.

print too many copies of a book before it knows how well it will sell. But by the time the fourth book, *The Battle of the Labyrinth*, was published, Disney Hyperion decided to start out by printing a whopping one million copies its first time off the printing presses.

It seems that Disney was right to print a lot of books. By mid-2011, Percy Jackson and the Olympians had been on the *New York Times* best-sellers list for children's book series for two hundred weeks. Each individual book in the five-book series also shot to number one on various best-sellers lists upon its release.

For fans of the series, there are also supplemental books to enjoy. *The Demigod Files* includes three original short stories about Percy Jackson, as well as a map of Camp Half-Blood. *Percy Jackson and the Olympians: The Ultimate Guide* is a handbook that goes along with the series and features character profiles and descriptions of the mythological characters, creatures, and monsters. It also includes maps, trading cards, and diagrams.

FOUR

BEYOND PERCY JACKSON

As the success of the Percy Jackson and the Olympians series was taking hold and enjoying significant time on best-sellers lists, Rick Riordan was doing anything but relaxing or resting on his laurels. He was hard at work on his next writing projects, each of which were in different stages of development. Each of these new book series, the 39 Clues, the Kane Chronicles, and Heroes of Olympus, are now enjoying their own success and share of the spotlight on the best-sellers lists.

THE 39 CLUES

The 39 Clues series was Riordan's next project after Percy Jackson, but it was not actually his idea. The idea was conceived by Scholastic Books, which approached Riordan to develop the concept into a series of books. In a July 2008 video interview for Scholastic's Web site, Riordan explained: "I didn't come up with the original idea for 39 Clues. Scholastic has some great people on their editorial team who came to me, and they said to me, 'Hey, we've got this idea and we're looking for somebody to turn it into a book and would you be interested?' And when they described the idea to me I said, 'Wow, that sounds really great. You get to do all this cool stuff with history and you get to make it like a scavenger hunt across the world.' So as a teacher myself for many years, I was really intrigued."

The series is about a brother and sister, Amy and Dan Cahill, who take on a challenge left in their grandmother's will. They can either have $1 million or find and use the thirty-nine clues that have been hidden around the world to unlock the secret of their family's mysterious and supreme power. Of course, the children take on the challenge.

Each book in the series relates to and features a different historical figure and international location. The first book in the series, *The Maze of Bones*, was written by Riordan and published in September 2008. It includes fascinating and intriguing historical information about Benjamin Franklin. Riordan wrote the story arc for all of the remaining ten books in the series, but the only other one he wrote was book

The *New York Times* bestselling series

VESPERS RISING

THE 39 CLUES™

RICK RIORDAN
PETER LERANGIS
GORDON KORMAN
JUDE WATSON

READ THE BOOKS. COLLECT THE CARDS. PLAY THE GAME.

The 39 Clues book series was created by Riordan along with Scholastic Books. Riordan came up with the idea for each book in the series and other authors helped write them.

eleven, *Vespers Rising*, with fellow 39 Clues authors Gordon Korman and Jude Watson. Each book in the series was published and released only a few months apart from each other. It would not have been possible for one writer to write all eleven books so quickly, especially given all the historical research the books required.

Each book in the 39 Clues series provides a clue to help the Cahills unlock their family secret, but the series has an interesting and innovative twist. Its storyline is continued through trading cards and an online game that help the reader find the other missing clues. Readers get trading cards with each book, and they can use these to go online and play the game, unlocking more clues along the way.

Riordan liked the educational aspect of the 39 Clues books. He explained in an interview published in the *New York Times* on September 1, 2008, "I saw 'the 39 Clues' as a potential vehicle for doing some education in a fun way—to take some of these amazing stories from history, dust them off and make them alive." As he wrote the series' first book, *The Maze of Bones*, Riordan hoped that it would have the same appeal to young people that Percy Jackson had. He explained in his video interview on Scholastic's Web site, "I wanted it to be really fast paced, I wanted it to have a sense of humor, a lot of action… I have two boys of my own and they don't

FROM THE *NEW YORK TIMES* #1 BEST-SELLING AUTHOR

RICK RIORDAN

The Kane Chronicles is yet another best-selling book series for Riordan. The first title in the three-book series, *The Red Pyramid,* was published in 2010.

like reading boring books, and I don't like writing boring books."

Riordan need not have worried. *The Maze of Bones*—and all subsequent installments of the series—was definitely appealing to young readers. The 39 Clues books also shot up to the top of bestsellers lists. The storyline is set to be adapted into a movie from Steven Spielberg's Dreamworks studio, with Spielberg as a producer and Brett Ratner as director. Ratner has directed other big-budget fantasy-adventure films such as the third X-Men film, *X-Men: The Last Stand*.

THE KANE CHRONICLES

Though Riordan had immensely enjoyed working on the 39 Clues series, it was not his own creation. The story idea had been presented to him, and he brought it to glorious life, along with other talented authors who worked to flesh out his story. Riordan's next project, however, would be all his, springing from his mind alone.

Riordan again returned to one of his favorite subjects: mythology. Instead of the Greek mythology that provided the narrative foundation for the Percy Jackson series, the new three-book Kane Chronicles series was inspired by Egyptian mythology. In this series, a brother and sister team, Carter and Sadie Kane, realize that their ancestors are powerful

THE MAGIC AND MYSTERY OF THE EGYPTIAN GODS

As the backdrop of the Kane Chronicles, ancient Egypt provides an interesting time period to learn about. Egyptian hieroglyphics, ancient magic, and the relationships among Egyptian gods all provide incredibly rich subject matter for the books. Below are some of the gods featured in the Kane Chronicles and their connection to authentic ancient Egyptian mythology.

- Isis is known as "the great mother." She can change her physical shape and is an expert at magic and healing.
- Set is also known by the name Seth. He is the god of evil and is often associated with desert sandstorms.
- Horus is a god with a falcon-shaped head. The son of Isis, Horus can ward off evil spirits. His eye has become a symbol of protection, and many sailors have painted the Eye of Horus on their ships for good luck.
- Anubis is the god of the dead. With the body of a human and the head of a jackal, his figure can often be seen protecting Egyptian tombs.
- Bes is the god that oversees and protects households, especially mothers and children. He is short and comical-looking, and his symbol is often used to safeguard homes.

Egyptian magicians. Egyptian gods are released into the modern world and wreak havoc. Carter and Sadie are the only ones who can defeat the gods and restore order. They set off on a global journey to save their father from Set, who is the god of evil, chaos, and darkness. The first book in the series, *The Red Pyramid*, was released in 2010. *The Throne of Fire* was published in 2011. The third and final book in the series, as yet untitled, will be published in the spring of 2012.

The Kane Chronicles are not only a fun read with a great story, they are also a highly entertaining way to learn a lot about history and mythology. On Riordan's Web site, readers can even find a student guide and event kit for *The Red Pyramid* produced by Disney Hyperion Books, the publisher of the series. The guide is filled with activities and ideas that supplement the book and help the reader learn more about ancient Egypt.

Riordan is very interested in getting his readers to become involved in history and learn more about it. As a former teacher, it is the same goal he always had for the students in his classroom. As he said in his 2008 interview with the *New York Times*: "I wanted my students to leave my classroom loving reading and wanting to read more, and if they left my classroom thinking that reading is boring,

The Kane Chronicles series is steeped in ancient Egyptian mythology, religion, and history. A party to celebrate the publication of *The Red Pyramid*, the first book in the series, was held at the Brooklyn Museum in New York City, which has an extensive collection of Egyptian art and artifacts.

then I haven't done my job." Keeping students interested in the topic is always important. As he said in the interview, "My goal in the classroom was always to make sure they were having so much fun that they didn't realize they were learning."

HEROES OF OLYMPUS

With all of the projects that Rick Riordan has worked on in the past few years, the Percy Jackson series has remained the most popular and in-demand by young audiences. So what better way to keep readers interested than to return to the world of Percy Jackson with Riordan's new five-book series, Heroes of Olympus? As he explains on his Web site, the series is not about Percy and it is not a repeat of the first series: "A story has to keep developing to be fresh, and if the author gets bored, the reader will get bored, too."

The series is set in the world of Percy Jackson, but the focus has shifted. The training camp that Percy attended, Camp Half-Blood, must be rebuilt after a battle with Kronos to save Olympus. The camp will be the place where the demigods who follow in Percy's wake will grow and train to live out their own quests and prophecies. Instead of focusing on Percy, Annabeth, and Grover, the adventures involve new characters, each with their own stories, talents, and connections to Greek mythology. The first book in the series, *The Lost Hero*, was released in the fall of 2010, and the second book, *The Son of Neptune*, came out in the fall of 2011. Each year, another book in the five-book series will be released until the series is complete in the fall of 2014.

Camp Half-Blood had been one of the more popular aspects of the Percy Jackson books. Riordan thought it would be a good idea to return to that unique setting to explore the adventures of other demigods. In fact, some young readers were so intrigued by Camp Half-Blood that local bookstores designed summer programs that were inspired by it. Bookstores in Austin, Texas; Decatur, Georgia; and Brooklyn, New York, started summer reading programs that honor the idea of Camp Half-Blood.

The Heroes of Olympus is a five-book series that Riordan is currently working on. It returns to Camp Half-Blood, the demigod training ground that was made popular in the Percy Jackson and the Olympians series, for a new round of adventures with a new cast of characters.

Riordan's biggest problem now is writing the books fast enough in his various ongoing, wildly popular series to satisfy eager and impatient readers. On his Web site, he assures these hungry readers that "I'm writing as fast as I possibly can without sacrificing quality. Normally it takes me one full year to write each book. I'm trying my best to speed that up, but it's a slow process to make a book and get it right. Readers will always be able to read faster than I can write."

So what comes after the Heroes of Olympus series? Riordan has mentioned in several interviews that he would be interested in writing a fictional series steeped in the Norse mythology that so inspired him as a child. However, he admitted it would be several years before he would have the time to think about and flesh out that idea. In the meantime, we can expect new books from Rick Riordan just about every year. Hopefully, that will be enough to satisfy his growing legion of clamoring fans.

RIORDAN ON WRITING

Millions of readers have found Rick Riordan's books to be fun, satisfying, engaging, and exciting. The books have inspired many students to read more, but they have also inspired others to want to become writers themselves. Riordan has given interviews in which he gives advice to students who want to become writers. Most times, he offers the same three tips.

EXPERT ADVICE

Riordan's first piece of advice to would-be authors is to read a lot. In an interview with Scholastic Books to promote the 39 Clues series, he explains that reading provides writers with inspiration, and it gives them useful examples of other authors who have written well and told compelling stories. Without reading, it would be much harder for someone to do a good job at writing. As Riordan advises on his Web site: "Read everything you can get your hands on. You will learn the craft of writing by immersing yourself in the voices, styles, and structures of writers who have gone before you."

The second piece of advice that Riordan gives to students who want to be authors is to write a little bit every day. He explains that, similar to exercising muscles to play a sport, it is also necessary to practice writing to exercise the writing "muscles." The more you write, the better you get, just as the more you practice a sport, the better you get at it. On his Web site, Riordan advises: "Keep a journal. Jot down interesting stories you heard. Write

One of Rick Riordan's tips for how to be a successful writer is to be an avid reader. Reading provides creative inspiration and good examples to follow. Books offer a hugely entertaining education in the art and craft of writing.

descriptions of people you see. It doesn't really matter what you write, but you must keep up practice. Writing is like a sport—you only get better if you practice. If you don't keep at it, the writing muscles atrophy."

The third piece of advice that Riordan gives about writing is to never give up. He explains that everyone feels bad after getting a rejection letter from a publisher, but it happens to all writers. If people gave up after their first rejection, there would be very few books for us to read. He encourages students to keep going, not give up, believe in themselves, and just keep trying to do what they enjoy. As he explains on his Web site, "Rejection is a part of writing, and it hurts. The trick is to keep at it. Wallpaper your room with rejection notes, if you want, but don't give up."

THE WRITING PROCESS

Writing can often be an overwhelming task, especially for people who are new at it and do not have much experience. The writing process can involve a lot of prewriting, which is thinking about your topic, researching it, and organizing your thoughts and content. Since Riordan's books are so thoroughly steeped in mythology and history, the prewriting stage, especially research, is especially important to

GET FEEDBACK

Good writers get feedback from trusted and respected readers so that they can tell if their writing is on the right track. When getting feedback about writing, remember that it is meant to help and that you should not be too sensitive. Rick Riordan took a chance and got feedback from his sons and some of his students after he wrote his first children's book, *The Lightning Thief*. The students provided constructive criticism, but instead of feeling discouraged, Riordan used the advice to improve his story.

When you receive feedback, you may have to go back to your story and rewrite some of it. Rewriting is a critical and indispensable component of good writing. Choose someone you trust to give you feedback, such as a mentor. But also think about the audience for whom you are writing. Ask someone who belongs to this target group to read and comment upon your work, just as Riordan asked middle school students to read his novel-in-progress.

him and to the eventual writing of a successful and convincing novel.

In an interview with Scholastic Books to promote the 39 Clues series, Riordan explained that it was important to do a lot of research before writing the

Riordan poses in front of a Benjamin Franklin statue in lower Manhattan. Franklin is one of the main inspirations for the plotline of the first book in the 39 Clues series.

first 39 Clues book, *The Maze of Bones*. He did a lot of reading about Benjamin Franklin because he knew that would be an important part of the story. Riordan explained that even though he was a history teacher and taught about Franklin in class, he still did a lot of reading and researching to discover new and interesting facts that could be used in the book.

After choosing the most intriguing and compelling facts to build the narrative around, Riordan began to outline the story. The outlining process clarifies a writer's thinking about the story he or she wants to tell and how it should be told. It also helps impose a structure on the story, organizing the sequence of scenes and events in the narrative arc and creating a satisfying pace from beginning to middle to end.

In the Scholastic interview, Riordan explained the process he goes through to write a book and keep the words and ideas flowing freely. "What I like to do is outline what I am going to say first, and that keeps me from getting writer's block." Authors find writer's block—the inability to find the words or ideas needed to write—to be one of the most difficult challenges to overcome when creating a piece. That is why Riordan feels it is important to get your ideas down, whether you like them or not. He explains of the writing process: "I'll sit down and I'll do the entire rough draft without making myself stop. That's the biggest problem that I had when I started writing, is that I would think that I had to revise as I went and that every chapter had to be perfect before I could write the next one. That didn't work for me at all. I never got past chapter three. So instead I just write the whole thing, even if I think it is terrible, I write the entire draft, and then I go back and I spend most of the rest of the year outlining through and making sure all the revisions work and just revising and revising and revising until I've got it the way I want it."

As many other writers also claim, an important part of writing for Riordan is the rewriting process. If there is nothing down on the page in the first place, it would not be possible to make revisions or move forward with the writing process. You would be stuck at the beginning for too long. This can get a writer frustrated and not allow ideas to flow. If ideas and words don't flow, no matter how flawed and in need of eventual revision they may be, writer's block can set in.

Riordan also explains that different books can take different amounts of time to complete. He says that the average amount of time he requires to complete a novel is anywhere from a few months to a few years. He says that *The Maze of Bones* took only a few months to write, but some other books have taken much longer.

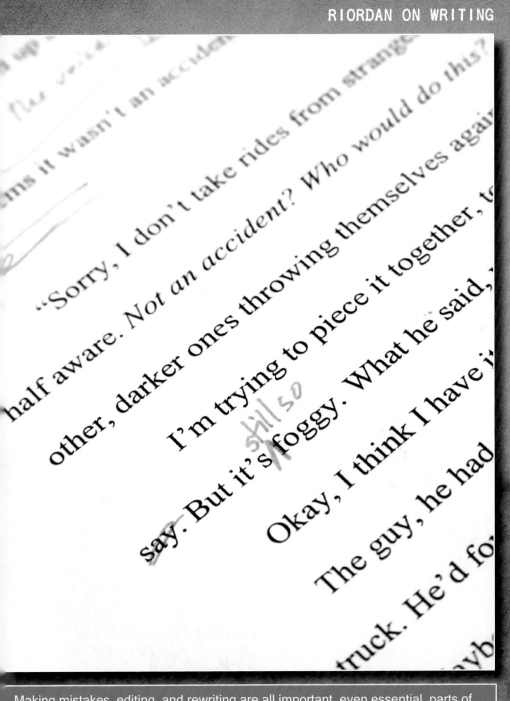

a up
the voice
ms it wasn't an accident

"Sorry, I don't take rides from strange

half aware. *Not an accident? Who would do this?*

other, darker ones throwing themselves agai

I'm trying to piece it together, t

say. But it's *still so* foggy. What he said,

Okay, I think I have j

The guy, he had

truck. He'd fo

yb

Making mistakes, editing, and rewriting are all important, even essential, parts of the writing process, according to Rick Riordan.

MAKE MISTAKES

As most writers will tell you, it is important to let yourself make mistakes when writing. Especially if you are writing down your ideas in hopes of avoiding writer's block, you have to accept that you will be making some mistakes along the way. As Riordan explains in an interview with Scholastic Books, "Writing is all about mistakes. You can't write without making mistakes." He also states: "Sometimes the mistakes are things you can really learn from. The biggest mistake, I think, is thinking that it has to be perfect. It doesn't have to be perfect. You can make it perfect later. The most important thing is to get your story onto the computer screen. Or onto the paper, first. Let yourself have permission to make mistakes the first time. In class, we used to call it a rough draft, or a sloppy copy. It's the same thing when you're writing a novel. Just go for it and get it down on paper. Then you can correct it all you want."

What kinds of mistakes might a writer make when writing a first draft? The most common might be spelling or grammar. Others include problems in a story. Perhaps you forgot to introduce a new character in your story. Or perhaps you introduced a character twice instead of just the first time he or she is mentioned in the story. These are mistakes that should be caught when you are revising your work. It takes a good editor—someone other than the author—with an eagle eye to catch every error in a piece of writing. But every writer should be able to review his or her own work, find some of the errors that need to be corrected, and make sure the writing is as clear and clean as possible.

FOR THE LOVE OF WRITING

During a speech given at the Rocky Mountain Fiction Writers Conference in Denver, Colorado, in 2006, Riordan talked about some of the things that people often ask him about writing. He said that many people tell him that they wish they could become writers to make money. He explained to the audience that he wouldn't be able to explain to people how he was able to become a full-time writer, much less explain how they could do it. He warned that it could take a very long time to have such a wish come true.

Riordan cautioned, "It took me ten years before I became a full-time writer, and even then I didn't plan it." He said that the desire to quit one's day job and make a lot of money should not be a reason to start writing books. The vast majority of would-be writers do not get published, and even those that do rarely get rich. The reason why people should start to write is because they enjoy it, have a passion for it, and

Riordan suggests that people who want to become writers should do it simply because they love doing it, not because they expect fame or fortune.

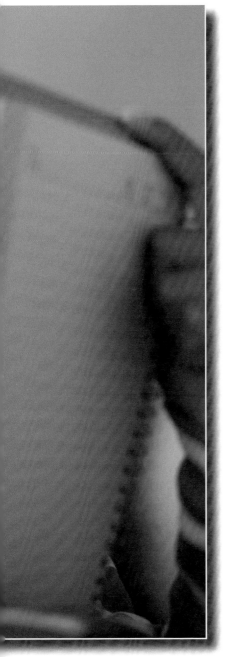

can't imagine not doing it. The pleasure of writing should be an end in itself, apart from any possible fame or publishing or financial success. It should be something you enjoy doing in your spare time, such as a sport or other hobby.

Finding the time to write, whether writing is one's job or a favorite hobby, is one of an author's greatest challenges. "A question I got asked constantly when I was a teacher," he told the conference of writers, was "'How do you possibly find the time to write?'" Just as many people have trouble finding extra free time, so did Riordan. He just wrote because he knew it was something he wanted to do. "I didn't have a good answer," he told the crowd. "I simply found the time because I had to. I would write in the early morning and again at night. I wrote about three or four hours a day, maximum. When I quit teaching, I had illusions that I'd get twice as much done. In fact, I still write about three to four hours a day. That seems to be my maximum output. I feel just as busy now as I ever have."

Writers should write the kind of book they would like to read, whether or not they are writing for children, young adults, or adults. Riordan believes that the elements that make a good adult book are the same elements that make a good children's book. He states on his Web site: "You know, when I was writing Percy Jackson, I didn't find it much different than writing an adult Tres Navarre novel. I think kids want the same thing from a book that adults want— a fast-paced story, characters worth caring about, humor, surprises, and mystery."

For Riordan, the most important requirement for a novel is to both provoke and satisfy the reader's curiosity: "A good book always keeps you asking questions, and makes you keep turning pages so you can find out the answers." By this criterion, Rick Riordan has provided his readers with many very, very good books. Hopefully, his ever-growing legion of fans will enjoy many more of his good books in the years ahead.

ON RICK RIORDAN

Birth date: June 5, 1964

Birthplace: San Antonio, Texas

Current residence: San Antonio, Texas

First adult book publication: *Big Red Tequila*, 1997

First children's book publication: *The Lightning Thief*, 2005

Marital status: Married

Children: Two sons, Haley and Patrick

College attended: University of Texas, Austin (bachelor's degree in English and history), and University of Texas, San Antonio (teacher's degree)

Awards: St. Mary Hall's Master Teacher Award; Shamus Award (*Big Red Tequila*); Anthony Award (*Big Red Tequila*); Edgar Award (*The Widower's Two-Step*); Mark Twain Award (*The Lightning Thief*; *The Sea of Monsters*); Rebecca Caudill Award (*The Lightning Thief*)

Film adaptations: *The Lightning Thief* (20th Century Fox; 2010)

ON RICK RIORDAN'S WORK

Percy Jackson and the Olympians series (published by Disney-Hyperion)

The Lightning Thief	2005
The Sea of Monsters	2006
The Titan's Curse	2007
The Battle of the Labyrinth	2008
The Last Olympian	2009
The Demigod Files (stories related to the Percy Jackson series)	2009

The 39 Clues series (published by Scholastic)

The Maze of Bones	2008
Vespers Rising	2011

The Kane Chronicles series (published by Hyperion)

The Red Pyramid	2010
The Throne of Fire	2011
The Serpent's Shadow	2012

Heroes of Olympus series (published by Hyperion)

The Lost Hero	2010
The Son of Neptune	2011

The Mark of Athena	2012
As-yet untitled fourth book in series	2013
As-yet untitled fifth book in series	2014

Tres Navarre books (adult detective fiction; published by Bantam)

Big Red Tequila	1997
Widower's Two-Step	1998
The Last King of Texas	2000
The Devil Went Down to Austin	2001
Southtown	2004
Mission Road	2005
Rebel Island	2007

Percy Jackson and the Olympians series
The Lightning Thief

"Perfectly paced, with electrifying moments chasing each other like heartbeats."—*New York Times Book Review*

"An adventure quest with a hip edge."—*School Library Journal* (starred review)

"Packed with humorous allusions to Greek mythology…along with rip-snorting action sequences, [this] book really shines."—*Horn Book Magazine*

> A *New York Times* Notable Book of 2005
> A *Child Magazine* Best Book of the Year
> A *School Library Journal* Best Book of the Year
> A *Today Show Book Club* Pick

The Sea of Monsters

"In a feat worthy of his heroic subjects, Riordan crafts a sequel stronger than his compelling debut."
—*Publishers Weekly* (starred review)

"[A] fast and funny tale, full of action, wisecracks, and superhuman powers."—*Kliatt* (starred review)

> A *Book Sense* Best Seller
> A *Book Sense* Top Ten Summer Pick for 2006
> A *Child Magazine* Best Book of the Year

The Titan's Curse

"All in all, a winner of Olympic proportions."—*School Library Journal*

A *USA Today* National Best Seller

The Battle of the Labyrinth

"Look no further for the next Harry Potter; meet Percy Jackson, as legions of fans already have." —*Kirkus Reviews* (starred review)

"The wit, rousing swordplay, and breakneck pace will once again keep kids hooked."—*Publishers Weekly* (starred review)

"The cliff-hanger ending will leave readers breathless in anticipation of the fifth and final volume."—*School Library Journal*

The Last Olympian

"The clash of modern and classical worlds is both exciting and entertaining."—*New York Times Book Review*

"Riordan masterfully orchestrates the huge cast of characters and manages a coherent, powerful tale at once exciting, philosophical, and tear-jerking. The best-selling series' legions of fans will cheer their heroes on and rejoice in such a compelling conclusion to the saga." —*Kirkus Reviews* (starred review)

The 39 Clues series
The Maze of Bones
"[T]ons of fun. Lead-off hitter Riordan mixes just the right proportions of suspense, peril and puzzles in a fast-paced...rollicking good read." —*Publishers Weekly* (starred review)

"Adeptly incorporating a genuine kids' perspective, the narrative unfolds like a boulder rolling downhill and keeps readers glued to the pages. As the siblings work together to solve puzzles and survive dangers, they develop into well-drawn individuals with their own strengths and personalities... [B]reathless fun. The book dazzles with suspense, plot twists, and snappy humor, but the real treasure may very well be the historical tidbits buried in the story. [T]his novel stands solidly on its own feet and will satisfy while whetting appetites for more." —*School Library Journal* (starred review)

The Kane Chronicles series
The Red Pyramid
"Riordan takes the elements that made the Percy Jackson books so popular and ratchets them up a notch...He has a winning formula, but this book

goes beyond the formulaic to present a truly original take on Egyptian mythology. His trademark humor is here in abundance, and there are numerous passages that will cause readers to double over with laughter. The humor never takes away from the story or from the overall tone. A must-have book, and in multiple copies."—*School Library Journal* (starred review)

"The first volume in the Kane Chronicles, this fantasy adventure delivers what fans loved about the Percy Jackson and the Olympians series: young protagonists with previously unsuspected magical powers, a riveting story marked by headlong adventure, a complex background rooted in ancient mythology, and wry, witty twenty-first-century narration. The last pages contain a clever twist that will leave readers secretly longing to open their lockers at the start of school."—*Booklist* (starred review)

The Heroes of Olympus series
The Lost Hero

"This book will delight fans of *The Lightning Thief* as Percy, Annabeth, and others play roles in the new prophecy and its subsequent quest...Riordan excels at clever plot devices and at creating an urgent sense of cliff-hanging danger."—*School Library Journal*

"Readers longing for a return to Camp Half-Blood will get their wish in the first novel of the Heroes of Olympus series, which follows Riordan's popular Percy Jackson and the Olympians series and includes some of the same characters in minor roles. Flashes of humor lighten the mood at times, but a tone of urgency and imminent danger seems as integral to this series as the last. With appealing new characters within a familiar framework, this spin-off will satisfy the demand for more."—*Booklist*

The Son of Neptune

"From the Roman demigod camp to the prison of Death himself, *The Son of Neptune* reunites readers with old friends and introduces them to a whole new cast of characters. The Roman camp is a far cry from Camp Half-Blood, but it's every bit as fascinating to explore…Rick Riordan is a master at balancing just the right amount of seriousness and levity in every situation, and his three teen narrators point out the strangeness of the iterations of ancient myths in the modern world with spot-on accuracy. With page-turning adventure, witty dialogue, and fun, fascinating characters, this second installment of the Heroes of Olympus series is a must-read for any fan of myths and fables."—Amazon.com Amazon Best Books of the Month October 2011

1964 Born in San Antonio, Texas.

1977 Receives rejection letter for first short story; becomes interested in Norse mythology.

1982 Graduates from Alamo Heights High School.

1986 Graduates from University of Texas, Austin, with a degree in both English and history.

1987 Gets teaching degree and moves to San Francisco.

1994 Finishes writing first adult novel, *Big Red Tequila*.

1997 First book, *Big Red Tequila,* is published.

1998 *Big Red Tequila* wins the Shamus Award and the Anthony Award.

1999 *The Widower's Two-Step* wins the Edgar Award.

2002 Awarded St. Mary Hall's first Master Teacher Award for his work at this San Antonio private school.

2005 *The Lightning Thief* is published.

2006 *The Sea of Monsters* is published.

2007 *The Titan's Curse* is published.

2008 *The Maze of Bones* and *The Battle of the Labyrinth* are published; *The Lightning Thief* wins the Mark Twain Award.

2009 *The Last Olympian* and *The Demigod Files* are published; *The Sea of Monsters* wins the Mark Twain Award; *The Lightning Thief* wins the Rebecca Caudill Award.

2010 *The Lost Hero* and *The Red Pyramid* are published; the film adaptation of *The Lightning Thief* is released.

2011 *The Son of Neptune, Vespers Rising*, and *The Throne of Fire* are published.

2012 *The Mark of Athena* is published.

TIMELINE

ADAPTATION The process of making something suitable for a new purpose, such as making a book suitable to be presented as a film.

ANCIENT Having an existence of many years; relating to a remote time or period in history.

ATTENTION DEFICIT/HYPERACTIVITY DISORDER (ADHD) A behavioral disorder that occurs mainly in children, causing poor concentration, overactivity, and impulsive behavior.

CAPTIVATE To influence and dominate by some special charm, art, or trait with an irresistible appeal.

DEMIGOD A being in mythology that is the offspring of a god and a mortal; a half-divine, half-human being.

DEVOUR To consume hungrily and greedily; to take in greedily with the eyes or mind.

DISABILITY Something that restricts; a limitation; a disadvantage.

DRAFT The first version, or early version, of a piece of writing.

DYSLEXIA A disorder that affects a person's ability to accurately interpret words, letters, numbers, or other symbols.

EPIC Extending beyond the usual or ordinary, especially in size or scope.

FANTASY GENRE A type of writing that uses characters or monsters with magical or supernatural powers and has settings and characters that could not exist in real life.

FEEDBACK Criticism, reaction, or comments about someone's work.

GERMANIC Relating to the language of Germany and its

speakers, as well as its folkloric and literary culture.

HERCULEAN Having the great size, strength, or courage of Hercules; very powerful or courageous; requiring great size, strength, or courage; something that is very difficult to do.

INNOVATIVE Introducing new methods; newly introduced; changing the way things are done.

INSPIRATION The process of being mentally stimulated and motivated to do something creative.

INSTALLMENT One of several parts (as of a publication) presented at intervals; one part of a serial story.

INTRIGUING Exciting interest or curiosity; fascinating.

LITERARY Related to literature and books; characterized by formal and polished language.

LITERATURE Imaginative writing, whether prose or poetry, especially that considered to have a lasting or permanent value, excellence of form, and strong emotional effect on the reader.

MEDIOCRE Ordinary; average; neither very good, nor very bad.

MENTOR An experienced adviser or role model who can teach or train someone in a particular area of skill or interest.

MYTHOLOGY A collection of myths, or traditional stories about the history of a culture, usually involving characters with supernatural powers.

NORSE Relating to the Scandinavian group of languages and culture.

OTHERWORLDLY Being apart from material things or earthly interests; spiritual or concerned with life in a future or imaginary world.

RELUCTANT Feeling or showing aversion, hesitation, or unwillingness.

SAGA A long story of adventure and heroic deeds.

SCANDINAVIAN Relating to the languages, peoples, and culture of Iceland, Norway, Sweden, and Denmark.

SCREENPLAY A story written for production as a film.

SOLITARY Being, living, or going alone or without companions; not social or gregarious (group-oriented).

SUBMISSION The act of sending or presenting something (such as a manuscript) for consideration or inspection; something that is presented for consideration or inspection.

TRILOGY A set of three related novels (or plays, films, albums, etc.) that together form an extended unified work.

YOUNG ADULT A category of literature that appeals specifically to teenagers.

Alliance for Young Artists & Writers
557 Broadway
New York, NY 10012
Web site: http://www.artandwriting.org
The Alliance for Young Artists & Writers is a nonprofit
    organization that identifies teens with artistic and
    literary talent and showcases their work and
    provides awards and scholarships.

Amazing Kids! Magazine
20126 Ballinger Way, NE, Suite 239
Shoreline, WA 98155
(206) 331-3807
Web site: http://www.amazing-kids.org
This kid-created online magazine and Web site help
    kids realize their creative potential.

The Center for the Book
Library of Congress
101 Independence Avenue SE
Washington, DC 20540-4920
(202) 707-5221
Web site: http://www.read.gov/cfb
The Center for the Book was established by the Library
    of Congress and now exists in all fifty states to
    promote reading and literacy.

DogEared
National Geographic Kids—Digital Media
1145 17th Street NW
Washington, DC 20036

This blog about books features reviews, recommenda-
tions, opinions, and wish lists written by kids.

Kenyon Review Young Writers Workshop
Finn House
102 West Wiggin Street
Kenyon College
Gambier, OH 43022
(740) 427-5208
Young Writers is an intensive two-week workshop for
intellectually curious, motivated high school
students who value writing. Its goal is to help
students develop their creative and critical abilities with language—to become better, more
productive writers and more insightful thinkers.
The program is sponsored by the *Kenyon
Review*, one of the country's preeminent literary
magazines.

Merlyn's Pen
Fiction, Essays, and Poems by America's Teens
11 South Angell Street, Suite 301
Providence, RI 02906
(800) 247-2027
Web site: http://www.merlynspen.org
Since 1985, Merlyn's Pen has supported teachers
who promote creativity, critical thinking, and
writing. Through its classroom magazines, teaching guides, instructional workbooks, audiotapes,
staged readings, writing contests, and summer-
and distance-learning programs, it has touched

the lives of millions of students in America. Its most public service since 2003 has been the New Library of Young Adult Writing, which showcases outstanding works of fiction and nonfiction authored by America's teens, grades six through twelve. Literature in the New Library inspires beginning writers. To advanced teen writers, the Library is an online resource of successful models to explore, engage, and emulate. When discussed in secondary classrooms, this literature sparks critical thinking and discussion about topics important in teen life.

Metropolitan Museum of Art
1000 Fifth Avenue
New York, NY 10028
(212) 535-7710
Web site: http://www.metmuseum.org
The Metropolitan Museum of Art has recently reopened its renovated and newly installed Greek and Roman Galleries, displaying thousands of beautiful masterworks, including stone and bronze sculptures, ceramics, glass, jewelry, wall paintings, and architectural elements. The collection of Greek and Roman art at the Metropolitan Museum—more than seventeen thousand works ranging in date from the Neolithic period to the time of the Roman emperor Constantine's conversion to Christianity in 312 CE—includes the art of many cultures and is among the most comprehensive in North America.

Midlink Magazine
SAS Campus Drive
Cary, NC 27513
(919) 531-2869
Web site: http://www.ncsu.edu/midlink
The mission of *MidLink Magazine* is to highlight
   exemplary work from the most creative classrooms around the globe. All content must be
   original, must enhance learning, and come
   directly from a classroom.

National Council of Teachers of English (NCTE)
Achievement Awards in Writing
1111 West Kenyon Road
Urbana, IL 61801-1096
Web site: http://www.ncte.org
The NCTE is devoted to improving the teaching and
   learning of English and the language arts at all
   levels of education. NCTE's Achievement
   Awards in Writing is a school-based writing
   program established in 1957 to encourage high
   school students in their writing and to recognize
   publicly some of the best student writers in the
   nation. It gives achievement awards in writing to
   students nominated and cited as excellent
   writers by judges.

National Writer's Association
10940 South Parker Road, #508
Parker, CO 80134

(303) 841-0246
Web site: http://www.nationalwriters.com
The National Writer's Association is a nonprofit organization that provides education and resources for
writers of differing levels of experience.

Scholastic Art & Writing Awards
Alliance for Young Artists & Writers
557 Broadway
New York, NY 10012
Web site: http://www.artandwriting.org
The Alliance for Young Artists & Writers, a nonprofit
organization, identifies teenagers with excep-
tional artistic and literary talent and brings their
work to a national audience through the
Scholastic Art & Writing Awards.

Skipping Stones
A Multicultural Children's Magazine
P.O. Box 3939
Eugene, OR 97403
(541) 342-4956
Web site: http://www.skippingstones.org
Skipping Stones is an award-winning nonprofit magazine for youth that encourages communication,
cooperation, creativity, and celebration of cultural
and environmental richness. It provides a playful
forum for sharing ideas and experiences among
youth from different countries and cultures.
Skipping Stones welcomes art and original

writings in every language and from all ages. In a typical issue, readers will find poems, stories, articles, and photos from many regions of the United States and the world.

Stone Soup
The Magazine by Young Writers and Artists
P.O. Box 83
Santa Cruz, CA 95063
(800) 447-4569
Web site: http://www.stonesoup.com
Stone Soup is the publication of the Children's Art Foundation. Since its founding in 1973, the foundation has become the leading publisher of children's writing and art in the English-speaking world. Its magazine, by young writers and artists is published in Santa Cruz, California. As the leading print magazine for children's creative writing for nearly forty years, *Stone Soup* is a fixture in many schools, libraries, and households.

TeenInk
P.O. Box 30
Newton, MA 02461
(617) 964-6800
Web site: http://www.teenink.com
TeenInk is a national teen magazine, book series, and Web site devoted entirely to teenage writing, art, photos, and forums. Students must be age thirteen to nineteen to participate, register and/

or submit work. Distributed through classrooms by English teachers, creative writing teachers, journalism teachers, and art teachers around the country, TeenInk offers some of the most thoughtful and creative work generated by teens and has the largest distribution of any publication of its kind.

Teen Voices
80 Summer Street, Suite 300
Boston, MA 0211o
(617) 426-5505
Web site: http://www.teenvoices.com
The mission of *Teen Voices* is to support and educate teen girls to amplify their voices and create social change through media. *Teen Voices* was founded in 1988 by two young women in Cambridge, Massachusetts, who believed in the power of girls and young women to create social change through writing and art. Their vehicle of choice was the production and publication of *Teen Voices*, a magazine by, for, and about teen girls.

Weekly Reader Publishing
Weekly Reader's Student Publishing Contest
3001 Cindel Drive
Delran, NJ 08075
(800) 446-3355
Web site: http://www.weeklyreadcr.com
Weekly Reader's Student Publishing Contest honors

the nation's best writing by students in grades three to twelve. Individual pieces, as well as print and online student publications, are eligible. Winners receive a free trip to Washington, D.C., plus other prizes.

Young Writers Project (YWP)
Champlain Mill
20 Winooski Falls Way, Suite #4
Winooski, VT 05404
(802) 324-9537
Web site: http://youngwritersproject.org
The YWP is a nonprofit formed in 2006 that engages thousands of students in grades three through twelve in a variety of writing projects and helps them improve and present their best work online, in newspapers, and on radio and stage through a variety of media and arts partners. It is committed to the idea that strong writing skills are critical for students to succeed, develop positive self-images, express themselves, and engage fully in their communities. Students with strong writing skills learn more and, later, are more apt to be hired or promoted in the workplace. YWP's vision is to create generations of confident writers and engaged citizens. Its mission is to reach as many students as possible, particularly those from socially and economically challenged backgrounds.

WEB SITES

Due to the changing nature of Internet links, Rosen Publishing has developed an online list of Web sites related to the subject of this book. This site is updated regularly. Please use this link to access the list:

http://www.rosenlinks.com/AAA/Rio

Brant, E. *She's All That!: A Look-It-Up Guide to the Goddesses of Mythology*. London, England: Franklin Watts, 2009.

Bryant, Megan E. *Oh My Gods!: A Look-It-Up Guide to the Gods of Mythology*. London, England: Franklin Watts, 2009.

Colum, Padraic. *The Golden Fleece and the Heroes Who Lived Before Achilles*. New York, NY: Random House Books for Young Readers, 2010.

Dickerson, Matthew T., and David L. O'Hara. *From Homer to Harry Potter: A Handbook on Myth and Fantasy*. Grand Rapids, MI: Brazos Press, 2006.

Evans, Lady Hestia, and Dugald A. Steer. *Mythology*. Somerville, MA: Candlewick Press, 2007.

Green, Roger Lancelyn. *Tales of the Greek Heroes*. New York, NY: Puffin, 2009.

Grimes, Heilan Yvette. *The Norse Myths*. Boston, MA: Hollow Earth Publishing, 2010.

Kass, Mallory. *The 39 Clues: The Black Book of Buried Secrets*. New York, NY: Scholastic, 2010.

Kelly, Sophia. *What a Beast!: A Look-It-Up Guide to the Monsters and Mutants of Mythology*. London, England: Franklin Watts, 2009.

Knight, Mary-Jane. *Percy Jackson and the Olympians: The Ultimate Guide*. New York, NY: Hyperion, 2010.

Lunge-Larson, Lise, and Gareth Hinds. *Gifts from the Gods: Ancient Words of Wisdom from Greek and Roman Mythology*. New York, NY: Houghton Mifflin Books for Children, 2011.

Martin, Philip. *A Guide to Fantasy Literature: Thoughts on Stories of Wonder and Enchantment*. Milwaukee, WI: Crickhollow Books, 2009.

Mendlesohn, Farah, and Edward James. *A Short History of Fantasy*. London, England: Middlesex University Press, 2009.

Napoli, Donna Jo. *Treasure of Greek Mythology: Classic Stories of Gods, Goddesses, Heroes, & Monsters*. Des Moines, IA: National Geographic Children's Books, 2011.

National Geographic. *National Geographic Essential Visual History of World Mythology*. Des Moines, IA: National Geographic, 2008.

O'Donoghue, Heather. *From Asgard to Valhalla: The Remarkable History of the Norse Myths*. New York, NY: I.B. Tauris & Co., Ltd., 2007.

Ollhoff, Jim. *Egyptian Mythology* (World of Mythology). Edina, MN: ABDO & Daughters, 2011.

Otfinoski, Steven. *All in the Family: A Look-It-Up Guide to the In-laws, Outlaws, and Offspring of Mythology*. London, England: Franklin Watts, 2009.

Philip, Neil. *Eyewitness Mythology*. New York, NY: DK Publishing, 2011.

Riordan, Rick. *The Kane Chronicles Survival Guide*. New York, NY: Hyperion, 2012.

Riordan, Rick, and Leah Wilson, eds. *Demigods and Monsters: Your Favorite Authors on Rick Riordan's Percy Jackson and the Olympians Series*. Dallas, TX: BenBella Books, 2009.

Roberts, Russel. *Poseidon: Profiles in Greek and Roman Mythology*. Hockessin, DE: Mitchell Lane Publishers, 2008.

Sturlson, Snorri, and Jesse L. Byock. *The Prose Edda: Norse Mythology*. New York, NY: Penguin Classics, 2006.

Tolkien, J. R. R. *The Fellowship of the Ring* (The Lord of the Rings). New York, NY: Mariner Books, 2005.

Tolkien, J. R. R. *The Hobbit*. New York, NY: Houghton Mifflin Harcourt, 2007.

Tolkien, J. R. R. *The Return of the King* (The Lord of the Rings). New York, NY: Mariner Books, 2005.

Tolkien, JRR *The Two Towers* (The Lord of the Rings). New York, NY: Mariner Books, 2005.

AdLit.org. "Transcript from an Interview with Rick Riordan." Retrieved July 2011 (http://www.adlit.org/transcript_display/29098/).

Borders Media Original Programming. "Rick Riordan." Retrieved August 3, 2011 (http://www.bordersmedia.com/liveat01/riordan).

Campbell, Joseph. *The Hero with a Thousand Faces*. Novato, CA: New World Library, 2008.

Campbell, Joseph. *The Masks of God, Volume 1: Primitive Mythology*. New York, NY: Penguin, 1991.

Campbell, Joseph. *The Masks of God, Volume 2: Oriental Mythology*. New York, NY: Penguin, 1991.

Campbell, Joseph. *The Masks of God, Volume 3: Occidental Mythology*. New York, NY: Penguin, 1991.

Campbell, Joseph. *The Power of Myth*. New York, NY: Anchor, 1991.

Camp Half-Blood Wiki. "Percy Jackson and the Olympians: *The Lighting Thief* Differences from the Book." Retrieved August 2011 (http://camphalf-blood.wikia.com/wiki/Percy_Jackson_and_the_Olympians:_The_Lightning_Thief/Differences_from_the_book).

Chaline, Eric. *The Book of Gods and Goddesses: A Visual Dictionary of Ancient and Modern Deities*. New York, NY: HarperCollins Publishing, 2004.

Clute, John, and John Grant. *The Encyclopedia of Fantasy*. New York, NY: St. Martin's Griffin, 1999.

FanPop.com. "Interview with Rick Riordan on May 3rd." Retrieved August 2011 (http://www.fanpop.com/spots/percy-jackson-and-the-olympians/articles/55366/title/interview-with-rick-riordan-on-may-3rd).

Johansen, K. V. *Quests and Kingdoms: A Grown-Up's Guide to Children's Fantasy Literature*. Sackville, NB, Canada: Sybertooth, Inc., 2005.

Knight, Mary-Jane. *Percy Jackson and the Olympians: The Ultimate Guide*. New York, NY: Hyperion, 2010.

Leeming, David Adams. *Oxford Companion to World Mythology*. New York, NY: Oxford University Press, 2009.

Lindow, John. *Norse Mythology: A Guide to Gods, Heroes, Rituals, and Beliefs*. New York, NY: Oxford University Press, 2002.

Lynn, Ruth. *Fantasy Literature for Children and Young Adults: A Comprehensive Guide*. Santa Barbara, CA: 2005.

McCarthy, Michael. *Masters of Imagination: Interviews with 21 Horror, Science Fiction, and Fantasy Writers and Filmmakers*. Duncan, OK: BearManor Media, 2010.

Memmott, Carol, Bob Minzesheimer, and Deirdre Donahue. "Book Buzz: Lightning Strikes for 'Percy Jackson' Sales." *USA Today*, January 24, 2010. Retrieved July 2011 (http://www.usatoday.com/life/books/news/2010-02-25-buzz25_ST_N.htm).

Mortalnet.com. "Rick Riordan Monopolizes the Top 5 Best Selling Books, on the *New York Times* Best Sellers List for Children's Chapter Books." Retrieved August 2011 (http://www.mortalnet.com/post/rick-riordan-monopolizes-the-top-5-best-selling-books-on-the-new-york-times-best-sellers-list-for-childrens-chapter-books).

NorseMythology.com. "Norse Mythology—Creation Story." Retrieved July 2011 (http://www.norse-mythology.com/Creation_Story.html).

Outlaw, Kofi. "Percy Jackson Sequel '*The Sea of Monsters*' in the Works." Screenrant.com. Retrieved August 2011 (http://screenrant.com/percy-jackson-sequel-the-sea-of-monsters-movie-kofi-104013).

Pinch, Geraldine. *Egyptian Mythology: A Guide to the Gods, Goddesses, and Traditions of Ancient Egypt.* New York, NY: Oxford University Press, 2004.

Rich, Motoko. "Author of Book Series Sends Kids on a Web Treasure Hunt." *New York Times,* September 1, 2008. Retrieved August 2011 (http://www.nytimes.com/2008/09/02/books/02rior.html).

RickRiordan.com. "Biography." Retrieved July 2011 (http://www.rickriordan.com/about-rick/biography.aspx).

RickRiordan.com. "Frequently Asked Questions." Retrieved July 2011 (http://www.rickriordan.com/about-rick/faq.aspx).

RickRiordan.com. "An Interview with Rick." Retrieved July 2011 (http://www.rickriordan.com/about-rick/an-interview-with-rick.aspx).

Rosenberg, Donna. *World Mythology: An Anthology of Great Myths and Epics.* 2nd ed. Chicago, IL: NTC Publishing Group, 1986.

Scholastic Videos: Author Interviews. "Rick Riordan Interview." Scholastic.com, July 2008.

Retrieved July 2011 (http://www2.scholastic.com/
browse/video.jsp?pID=1640183585&bcpid=16401
83585&bckey=AQ~~,AAAAAFv844g~,BASb5BU
03X_L2cn86MC9qSzQHunGEilJ&bclid=176864157
3&bctid=1770661250).

Stableford, Brian. *The A to Z of Fantasy Literature*.
Lanham, MD: Scarecrow Press, 2005.

The Stacks blog. "Percy Jackson Movie vs. Book."
Scholastic.com, November 28, 2009. Retrieved
August 2011 (http://blog.scholastic.com/ink_
splot_26/2009/11/percy-jackson-movie-vs-book
.html).

The39Clues.com. "About The 39 Clues." Retrieved
August 2011 (http://www.the39clues.com/info/
about).

Vejvoda, Jim. "Brett Ratner Uncovers the 39 Clues:
X-Men 3 Director to Take on Kid Lit Adaptation."
IGN.com, May 10, 2011. Retrieved August 2011
(http://movies.ign.com/articles/116/1167308p1
.html).

Weinman, Sarah. "Will 'Percy Jackson' Author Rick
Riordan Ever Reach J. K. Rowling Territory?"
DailyFinance.com, June 26, 2010. Retrieved August
2011 (http://www.dailyfinance.com/2010/06/26/
will-percy-jackson-author-rick-riordan-ever-reach-j-
k-rowling).

INDEX

ABOUT THE AUTHOR

Adam Furgang has been writing books for middle grade readers for many years. He has a degree in fine arts and has been writing fiction of his own. Like Rick Riordan, Furgang has a great interest in mythology and a son who is a big Percy Jackson fan.

PHOTO CREDITS